SCHOLASTIC

EASY SIMULATIONS

PIONEERS

by Tim Bailey

New York • Toronto • London • Auckland • Sydney
Mexico City • New Delhi • Hong Kong • Buenos Aires

Teaching
Resources

DEDICATION

This book is dedicated to my children, Alicia, Rachel, and Kyle.
To my wife, Jill, I am, as I ever was and ever shall be, yours.

ACKNOWLEDGMENTS

I would like to recognize Maria L. Chang for her incalculable help and guidance with this project
and to the rest of the amazing people that I have had the fortune to work with at Scholastic.

Editor: Maria L. Chang
Cover design by Jason Robinson
Cover illustration by Doug Knutson
Interior design by Holly Grundon
Interior illustrations by Eulala Conners

ISBN-13: 978-0-439-52220-5
ISBN-10: 0-439-52220-X
Copyright © 2008 by Tim Bailey
All rights reserved.
Printed in the U.S.A.

1 2 3 4 5 6 7 8 9 10   40   15 14 13 12 11 10 09 08

CONTENTS

Introduction

December 8, 1849

Dear Aunt Bertha,

. . . It was real hard most of the time. There wasn't just fun and games. A matter of fact there really wasn't any fun or games. It was really hard sometimes. I just thought we would die and given up hope.

This quote is taken from a letter, not by a real pioneer, but by a fifth-grade student who is role-playing a pioneer, writing to a fictional aunt at the end of our weeklong simulation. Using simulations in the classroom is one of the most powerful teaching methods you can choose. Students learn most when they see a purpose to an activity, are engaged in the learning process, and are having fun. Children love to role-play, and they do it naturally. How often have you overheard them say something like, "Okay, you be the bad guy, and I'll be the good guy"? Why not tap into students' imaginations and creativity and teach them by engaging them in a simulation?

What Is a Simulation?

A simulation is a teacher-directed, student-driven activity that provides lifelike problem-solving experiences through role-playing or reenacting. Simulations use an incredible range of effective teaching strategies. Students will acquire a richness and depth of understanding of history that's impossible to gain through the use of any textbook. They will take responsibility for their own learning, discover that they must work cooperatively with their team in order to succeed, and apply skills in math and logic to solve the problems that they encounter. You will find that this simulation addresses a variety of academic content areas and fully integrates them into this social studies activity. In addition, simulations motivate *all* of your students to participate because what they're required to do will be fully supported by their teammates and you. A non-English-speaking student wrote in Spanish in her pioneer journal: "I like to learn this way very much because I learn and work with my friends and it is like I am really there."

History Comes Alive

Easy Simulation: Pioneers is designed
to teach students about the westward
expansion by inviting them to relive a part
of that event. Over the course of five days,
they will re-create some of the experiences
of those brave individuals who settled the
American West. By taking the perspective of a
historical character living through the westward
journey, students will see that history is so much
more than just names, dates, and places, but rather the real experiences of people
like themselves.

Students will find out what it was like to be pioneers traveling with a wagon company in
1849 as it winds its way from Independence, Missouri, to the Willamette Valley of Oregon. They
will work together in groups and use their problem-solving skills to deal with challenges they
encounter as they cross the plains, journey to South Pass, and enter the Oregon Territory.

Throughout the simulation, students will keep a journal of their experiences and keep track
of the supplies they use and the distance they have traveled. At the end of the simulation, they
will write a letter to a fictional aunt who lives "back East," describing what they have experienced
and what they have learned from the activity. You can use both their journal and this letter as
assessment tools to determine what students have learned.

Everything You Need

This book provides an easy-to-use guide for running this five-day simulation—everything
you need to create an educational experience that your students will talk about for a very
long time. You will find background information for both yourself and your students, describing
the history and significance of the pioneer period. You'll also find authentic accounts—from
letters and journals written by people who experienced the same trials that your students will be
enduring—as well as maps, tables, illustrations, and reproducible student journal pages. There
are even some pioneer recipes at the back of this book that you can try with your class.

Before you begin the simulation, be certain to read through the entire book
so you can familiarize yourself with how a simulation works and prepare any materials
that you may need. Feel free to supplement with photos, illustrations, pioneer diaries,
videos, music, and any other details that will enhance the experience for you and your
students. Enjoy!

SETTING THE SCENE:
PIONEERS AND THE GREAT WESTERN MIGRATION

On April 30, 1803, Napoleon Bonaparte of France sold Thomas Jefferson, then President of the United States, 885,000 square miles of territory in North America for 15 million dollars. Congress then sent Meriwether Lewis and William Clark to explore this unfamiliar land that the United States had purchased. The Lewis and Clark expedition reached the Pacific Ocean on November 7, 1805, and the way to the West was opened. Fur trappers, traders, and finally pioneer settlers soon followed.

In 1841 the first group of 69 pioneers left Missouri and headed west, bound for Oregon. President James Polk soon declared that it was America's "manifest destiny" to settle North America from the Atlantic Ocean to the Pacific Ocean, and the people of America showed their agreement by pushing the borders of the United States across the Mississippi River and ever westward. From this time until the completion of the transcontinental railroad in 1869, more than 350,000 emigrants traveled by foot, handcart, and wagon to reach Oregon and California. At the peak of this westward migration more than 55,000 pioneers would make the hazardous crossing in a single season.

The 2,000-mile journey from Missouri to Oregon was not something to be undertaken lightly. It was a grueling five- to eight-month ordeal. One in every 17 people who began the trip died along the way. If pioneers' graves were evenly spaced along the Oregon Trail's 2,000-mile length, there would be a tombstone every 80 yards to mark the resting place of a traveler who

Easy Simulations: Pioneers © 2008 by Tim Bailey, Scholastic Teaching Resources

did not survive the journey. Lives were claimed by starvation, accidents, outlaws, hostile Native Americans whose lands were being invaded, and, perhaps most aggressively, by the dreaded disease cholera.

If the journey was so dangerous, why did so many pioneers risk their own lives and the lives of their families in order to make this migration? One of the most common reasons was the promise that there was something better out West than could be found in the East. In 1843 a trapper who had been to Oregon's Willamette Valley told a group of prospective emigrants that *"the pigs are running around about under the great acorn trees, round and fat, and already cooked, with knives and forks sticking in them so that you can cut off a slice whenever you are hungry."* Popular publications and guidebooks of the time boasted of Oregon's lush farmlands and California's goldfields. One book wrote that *"as far as its producing qualities are concerned Oregon can not be outdone whether in wheat, oats, rye, barley, buckwheat, peas, beans, potatoes, turnips, cabbages, onions, parsnips, carrots, beets, currants, gooseberries, strawberries, apples, peaches, pears, or fat and healthy babies."* Oregon seemed, from all accounts, to be paradise on Earth. All one had to do was get there and claim his little bit of heaven. It was that hope that made it worth the risks of the journey. To top it all off, the discovery of gold at Sutter's Mill in California in 1848 created a huge surge in the number of people choosing to emigrate to the West and try their luck in California.

While these reasons pulled people West, a number of factors pushed people out of the East. A series of financial crises that began in 1837 brought about a depression and ruined many farmers. In addition, several disease epidemics, including typhoid, dysentery, tuberculosis, scarlet fever, malaria, and yellow fever, were sweeping through many parts of the eastern United States. Perhaps the most devastating disease was cholera, which had arrived from Asia in the 1830s, and accounted for more than 50,000 deaths in 1850.

Other people chose to emigrate to the West for the same reason that many people came to the Atlantic shores of America two centuries before—religious freedom. Mormon pioneers, members of the Church of Jesus Christ of Latter-Day Saints, left Illinois in 1846 to find a place to practice their religion without fear of persecution and settled in the Salt Lake valley of Utah.

Adventurers, missionaries, land speculators, and many others followed the reasoning of Henry David Thoreau when he said, *"Eastward, I go only by force, but westward I go free . . . the prevailing tendency of my countrymen."*

Before You Start

Organizing and Managing the Simulation

Before students embark on their five-day journey, you will need to set the stage for the simulation. First, make photocopies of the reproducible pages at the end of this section:

- Traveling the Oregon Trail (pages 17–18)

- Choose a Role (page 19)

- A Pioneer's Diary (pages 20–21)

- Wagon Company Journal (pages 22–23)

- Wagon Supplies (pages 24–25)

- Rubrics (page 26)

- Simulation Spinner (page 27)

Explain to students that they will be re-creating history, using the simulation and their imaginations to learn what it was like to be pioneers during the westward expansion. They will be taking on the roles of various pioneers in that period and making the same decisions that those people made.

Distribute copies of "Traveling the Oregon Trail" to students. You might also want to reproduce the pages on transparencies to display on the overhead projector. As a class, read the selection to build students' background knowledge about the period they're about to live through. Then divide the class into groups of four or five students, with each group representing a wagon company that traveled across the country in 1849.

Choosing a Role

After you have divided the class into small groups, distribute the "Choose a Role" handout, which describes the various roles students can play during the simulation. Invite students to select a role from the handout, explaining that these "roles" were typical occupations in the mid-1800s. Each role comes with its own set of special skills and with strengths and weaknesses indicated by a number ranging from 1 to 5. These numbers are called "attributes." The higher the attribute number, the more able the character. (See Attributes, next page.)

Students have to pay special attention to the Health and Food attributes. The Health number shows how healthy a person is—5 is perfect health, and 1 is near death. Health can change throughout the simulation, depending on circumstances. The Food number, while technically not a real attribute, indicates how many pounds of food a pioneer consumes each day.

Encourage students within each group to choose a variety of roles to make the simulation more interesting. While any combination of pioneer roles is possible within each group, it may not be wise to have a group of, say, five doctors in one wagon company.

Attributes

Attributes are the numbers that make each pioneer role unique. The attributes are Strength, Common Sense, Hunting/Fighting Skills, Negotiation Skills, Medical Expertise, and Health. Throughout the simulation, attribute numbers will be used during "skill spins" to resolve various situations that the groups will encounter. Players will spin the spinner (or roll a die) and compare the number they've spun to their attribute number to determine whether their attempt at solving a problem is successful or not. For example, say a tree has fallen across the trail in the simulation. In order to move the tree, a wagon-company member (a student) must make a spin and compare that number to her Strength attribute. If the number she spins is equal to or lower than her Strength attribute, she has succeeded in moving the tree. If the number spun is higher, then she has failed.

Each group member is allowed only one skill spin per situation. In other words, if a student fails in her Strength spin she cannot attempt to move the tree again. Someone else in the wagon company would have to try his luck by making another Strength spin.

Below is a description of the various Attributes:

Strength: The physical strength of a person. This determines how easily a pioneer can perform tasks that require physical power.

Common Sense: A person's wisdom and ability to understand and reason. This can be very important in figuring out how to react to different situations and foreseeing problems.

Hunting/Fighting Skills: How skilled a pioneer is at hunting for food and at fighting using either a pistol or rifle.

Negotiation Skills: How well a character can reason with or influence other people. A good negotiator can get a better price or can defuse a dangerous situation, while a poor negotiator could end up insulting the person with whom he is talking.

Medical Expertise: How skilled a person is at caring for the sick and injured. A high number in this attribute could save the life of a fellow pioneer.

Health: A person's current health. All pioneers start with a Health of 5. During the simulation, a pioneer might lose a Health point due to sickness, injury, or starvation. If the Health number reaches zero, then that pioneer has died. The only way to regain lost Health points is to have someone else in the wagon company make a successful Medical Expertise spin; unless, that is, the loss of Health points is due to starvation. In this case, the Health points lost to starvation are restored when the pioneer gets food. Each scenario describes when a Medical Expertise spin may be made. If a pioneer dies at some point during the simulation then that student should still participate in group decisions and discussions as the "unseen conscious" of the wagon company. That student should still be expected to keep up his or her pioneer diary.

Other Important Features

Included in the table under "Choose a Role" are two features that are not actual attributes, but are nevertheless important in the pioneer experience:

Food: This number indicates how many pounds of food a person consumes every day. The Food number of every member in a wagon company will be added up to determine how much food will be subtracted from the company's supplies for each day of the journey.

One of the greatest challenges for students is having enough food to complete the journey. This was also the case for the real pioneers who made this trek. If the group runs out of food and they do not have the means to obtain more, either by buying it at a fort along the way or by hunting (see Hunting for Food, below), **each member will lose one Health point for every five days they go without food**. These Health points are restored once the wagon company gets more food. However, it is possible for a wagon company to starve to death.

Money: Each role brings with it a certain amount of money. Members of each wagon company pool their money to buy the wagon, food, and supplies they need for the journey.

Hunting for Food

During the course of the simulation, a wagon company may want or need to supplement their food supply by hunting for food along the way. To do this, they will need to spend the day hunting instead of traveling. A rifle and boxes of bullets are needed for every individual who wishes to attempt to hunt. To determine the success or failure of a hunter, that person must make a skill spin based on his or her Hunting/Fighting Skills.

If the designated hunter spins a number equal to or lower than his Hunting/Fighting number, the hunt was successful. The company then:

- subtracts one box of bullets from the wagon company's supply list; and

- spins the spinner and multiplies the number shown by 50 to determine how many pounds of food are gained.

If the hunter spins a number higher than his Hunting/Fighting number, the hunt was unsuccessful. A box of bullets is still subtracted from the supply list, but no food is gained.

For example, say a wagon company is down to 50 pounds of food and wishes to spend one day hunting. They have two guns and 10 boxes of bullets. The two people with the best Hunting/Fighting Skills try their luck. One fails, but the other succeeds. Two boxes of bullets are subtracted from the company's supply, leaving them with eight. The successful hunter spins a 5 and gains 250 pounds of food for the wagon company. Remind students to add any days spent hunting to their travel journals.

On the Hunt

- One day is used to go hunting.

- One rifle per hunter.

- One box of bullets is used per hunting attempt.

- The hunter's spin succeeds if she spins a number equal to or lower than her Hunting/ Fighting Skills number.

  → If the hunter succeeds, she spins again to see how much food is gained. Number spun × 50 = pounds of food gained.

  → If the hunter fails, then no food is gained.

Keeping a Journal

After students have chosen their roles, distribute copies of "A Pioneer's Diary"—one copy of the cover page and five copies of the blank "Dear Diary" page. Explain to students that they will be recording their experiences during the simulation in their diaries on a daily basis. To give the diaries a more realistic look, have students make a cover using a sheet of 12-by-18-inch brown construction paper or a large brown paper grocery bag. Demonstrate how to "sew" the diary pages inside the cover page using a hole punch and yarn, as shown.

On the cover page, have students fill in the information about the character they've chosen—the name, role, and attribute numbers. When students fill in their diary pages, have them record the date of the simulation, not the actual date. For example, use June 19, 1849, rather than November 6, 2008. Students should record the events that took place in that day's episode. Encourage them to write their diary entry "in character," as if the events had really happened to them. This activity gives students the opportunity to take on another person's perspective and experience history "firsthand."

A PIONEER'S DIARY

Pioneer's Name: Jeremy

Pioneer's Role: Farmer

Wagon Company's Name: The Westbound Trailers

Pioneer's Attributes:

Strength: 4

Common Sense: 4

Hunting/Fighting Skills: 3

Negotiation Skills: 2

Medical Expertise: 2

Health: 5

Pounds of food eaten per day: 3

Starting funds: $200

20
Easy Simulations: Pioneers

A student's diary often yields rich insights into the student's understanding of historical events and how they affected ordinary citizens' lives. Use these diaries as your primary tool for assessing students' participation and evaluating how well they understand the simulation's content. (See Assessing and Evaluating, page 15.)

In addition to their personal diaries, each wagon company will also keep a Wagon Company Journal, which lists the names and roles of each member and serves as a running record of the company's travel time, money, and supplies. **Students must keep track of the dates as this will determine their fate in Episode 5.** Encourage each group to decide upon a name for their wagon company, such as "The 'Oregon or Bust' Wagon Company." Group members should take turns recording in the Wagon Company Journal.

Getting Ready for the Journey

Before the actual simulation begins, students must outfit their party for the journey west. Members of a wagon company must combine their resources to buy their wagon, livestock for a wagon team, and the supplies they will need.

Distribute the "Wagon Supplies" list to students and discuss the different supplies and options available to them. After students clearly understand their task, they may proceed with buying their supplies. Remind students to record what they have bought in their Wagon Company Journal. They should also record how much food the company has and how much they will consume each day. Students should also calculate how much weight their wagon is carrying. (You may decide not to require younger students to keep track of the weight to simplify their bookkeeping and math.) There is also a place to record how much money the company has left for possible future expenses. (They'll be able to buy more supplies at forts along the way, but at double the prices.) Consider passing out calculators to students to help them with their calculations.

Below is an example of how a group might outfit their wagon. The group consists of a Doctor, a Scout, a Blacksmith, and a Hunter. Their combined resources amount to $850, and they decide to purchase the following:

- Prairie schooner $90   (will hold 2,500 lbs)
- 2 oxen teams $200
- Food $75   (300 lbs)
- Water barrel $4   (500 lbs)
- Cooking gear $8   (20 lbs)
- 2 spare wheels $50   (200 lbs)
- 1 spare yoke $10   (25 lbs)
- 2 rifles $100   (20 lbs)
- 10 boxes of bullets $30   (30 lbs)
- Blacksmith tools $40   (150 lbs)
- Seed $10   (50 lbs)
- Lantern $5   (5 lbs)

In their Wagon Company Journal, they record that they spent $622 and have $228 left. They also record that they loaded the wagon with 1,300 pounds of supplies. Finally, they record the fact that they will consume 12 pounds of food per day.

After all the preparations have been made to make the journey to Oregon, your students are ready to begin the simulation.

Conducting the Simulation

This simulation is divided into five episodes—one for each day of the school week—each re-creating the travels of pioneers as they journey from Independence, Missouri, to the Willamette Valley in Oregon. An episode should take about 45–60 minutes, depending on your class size. Consider starting the actual simulation on a Monday so that it will run its course by Friday. During the previous week, students should already have organized their wagon companies and learned the rules of the simulation.

Each episode consists of two scenarios, which feature problem-solving activities that simulate some of the difficulties and experiences that a westward-bound pioneer wagon company might have encountered in the mid-nineteenth century. How well students negotiate these challenges will determine their success or failure as pioneer homesteaders. After the wagon companies have reached their destination, students will engage in a discussion and debriefing of the simulation experience.

A Sample Scenario

The scenario presented in each episode is where students actually get to participate in a historical event. Below is an abbreviated version of a scenario in Episode 1: Wagons Ho! to demonstrate how a simulation scenario is typically run:

Read or paraphrase the opening scene in "Crossing Big Blue" (page 29), where pioneers have reached the Big Blue River and must now decide how to cross this deep, wide body of water. They have three choices:

1. Use the ferry to cross the river and pay the ferryman $15.

2. Ask the ferryman for another way to cross the river.

3. Float their wagon across the river.

Allow students within each group to discuss their next step, then invite a wagon-company spokesperson to present the group's decision. (Choose a different spokesperson from each group every day.)

> **Teacher:** Okay, has everyone had enough time to decide what they want to do? Wagon Company 1, what did you decide?
>
> **Wagon Company 1 Spokesperson:** We decided to pay the guy at the ferry.

Teacher: All right. (*Notes on a piece of paper that Wagon Company 1 will pay for the ferry*) Wagon Company 2?

Wagon Company 2 Spokesperson: Yeah, we'll do that too.

Teacher: You want to pay for the ferry as well? Okay. (*Notes that down as well*) Company 3?

Wagon Company 3 Spokesperson: We'd like to ask the ferryman for another way across the river.

Teacher: Okay.

Wagon Company 3 Spokesperson: Hey, is there another way across the river?

Teacher: (*deepening her voice to get into character*) "Why sure! You all can go south down to Alcove Springs and cross at the ford. Of course it's about 40 miles out of the way. Or you can try to float your wagon across right here."

Wagon Company 3 Spokesperson: (*After consulting with the rest of the wagon company*) We're going down to the ford. We don't want to spend the money to use the ferry, and floating across sounds too dangerous.

Teacher: Okay. (*Notes that Wagon Company 3 is going to the ford*) Wagon Company 4?

Wagon Company 4 Spokesperson: Can we negotiate a lower price for the ferry?

Teacher: Sure. (*Notes that Wagon Company 4 wants to negotiate*) Who is going to make a Negotiation Skills spin?

Wagon Company 4 Spokesperson: Our doctor; his Negotiation number is 3.

Teacher: Okay. Wagon Company 5, what do you want to do?

Wagon Company 5 Spokesperson: We like that idea. We'll negotiate too.

Teacher: Fine. (*Takes a note of this*) Who's doing the negotiating?

Wagon Company 5 Spokesperson: Our banker's Negotiation number is 5.

Teacher: Okay, everyone let's see what happens because of your decisions. Wagon Companies 1 and 2 subtract $15 from your money to pay for the ferry.

Wagon Company 3 you have traveled 40 miles to get to the ford and another 40 miles to get back to the trail on the other side of the river. Figure out how many days that took, adjust what date it is now for your wagon company, and subtract that many days' worth of food. [With two teams of oxen pulling their wagon, the company took eight extra days to cross the ford. So they must subtract eight days' worth of food from their supplies.]

Wagon Company 4 (*handing them the spinner*), you need to spin a 3 or lower. (*The wagon company's doctor spins a 2.*) Great! (*Going back into the ferryman persona*) "Well, I guess I'll let you go across for only $10. You seem like nice folks." Wagon Company 4, subtract $10 from your money.

Wagon Company 5 (*handing them the spinner*), you need to spin a 5 or less. (*The wagon company's banker spins a 6.*) Oh, bad luck! (*Going back into ferryman persona*) "Well, I never! Such uppity eastern folk! If you want to use my ferry it's gonna cost you $20!" What about it, Wagon Company 5? Pay the ferryman or choose to go down to the ford or float your wagon across . . .

This is how the scenarios will typically run, with role-playing students dealing with the situations that confront them along the Oregon Trail, and you, the teacher, acting out all the other parts while coordinating the simulation. You present the situation in the scenario to students and then give them time to make their decisions. You have to stay on your toes because students may come up with a solution different from those offered in the simulation. In such cases, you can either wing it and accommodate them or tell them that they must stick to the solutions offered in the simulation. Do not reveal the outcome of each student's or group's decision until everyone has responded; only then do you respond to each person or group as the rest of the class observes the outcome of the choices as scripted in the scenario.

Assessing and Evaluating

Throughout the unit students should be evaluated on their historical understanding. You can do this by assessing the authenticity and historical accuracy of the way they play their character and the diary entries they've written throughout this simulation.

Use the rubrics on page 26 to give each student a daily score, based on the student's diary entries and your observations. Each rubric is scored on a scale of 1 to 5, with 1 being the lowest possible score and 5 the highest. Add the two scores from Rubrics #1 and #2 to generate a number from 2 to 10. To convert this total score to a percentage score, multiply the total score by 10. You can award scores such as 4.5 if you feel a student was at least a 4 but not quite a 5. This daily percentage score can then be averaged over the week to generate a final grade for the simulation.

Another piece of the assessment puzzle is the group dynamic. This simulation is the perfect setting for teaching students the value of teamwork and collaboration. At the end of each day's simulation, as students are recording in their journals, debrief quickly with each group to discuss how they had worked together as a group. Were they patient with each other? Were they respectful of each other's opinions? Did the group dynamic feel supportive or combative? Based on this discussion, use Rubric #3 to record a group score for that day. At the end of the week, total the group score and then multiply by 4 in order to give the group a percentile score. After the simulation is finished, combine the group's scores with each member's daily scores to give each student a final grade for the simulation.

	Student Log		Teacher Observations		Score Percentage
Monday	3	+	4	x 10	70%
Tuesday	4	+	4	x 10	80%
Wednesday	3.5	+	5	x 10	85%
Thursday	2.5	+	4	x 10	65%
Friday	4	+	5	x 10	90%
Average for the week					78%

	Group's Daily Score
Monday	4
Tuesday	4
Wednesday	5
Thursday	3
Friday	5
Total	21 x 4 = 84%

A student with an individual score of 78% combined with his group score of 84% will get a final average score for the simulation of 81%, or a B.

TRAVELING THE OREGON TRAIL

The Oregon Trail

The Oregon Trail began in the town of Independence, Missouri, and stretched for 2,000 miles until it reached the Willamette Valley in western Oregon. Pioneers traversing this trail proved their bravery and resourcefulness by surviving—or simply enduring—the five- to eight-month journey.

These *emigrants*, as they were called, walked most of the way since their wagons had no room for passengers. The wagons carried everything they needed on the trail as well as everything they would need once they reached their new home. Only very small children or those too sick or injured to walk were allowed to ride with the driver in the wagon.

Much of what we know about what the journey was like—crossing rivers, prairies, and mountains to get to Oregon—came from the pioneers' daily journals and diaries. They tell us about using "buffalo chips" to cook with because there were no trees for firewood on the open prairie. These journals even tell how pioneer children discovered that dried buffalo dung made for a pretty good Frisbee! Pioneer Amelia Knight wrote in her diary about traveling on the Oregon Trail in 1853:

"Made our beds down in the tent in the wet and mud . . . Have to eat cold supper . . . We are creeping along slowly, one wagon after another, the same old gait; and the same thing over, out of one mud hole and into another all day . . . Them that eat the most breakfast eat the most sand . . . It has been raining all day long . . . we are a poor looking set, and all this for Oregon."

Although much of the journey was boring, at times it was filled with peril. Pioneers would sometimes have to float their wagons across rivers because there was no other way to cross. Prairie fires, wind, and violent storms were always a risk. And if the emigrants took too long to reach the mountains of Oregon, they faced blizzards and freezing cold as they tried to cross the Cascades. Some pioneers chose to try to float down the Columbia River to the Willamette Valley and brave the rapids rather than the snow. Native American Indians were usually not as great a threat as most pioneers feared, but there was occasional fighting between the pioneers and the tribes whose land they were crossing. One of the greatest dangers that any pioneer faced was catching cholera, which claimed the lives of many victims. Having enough food was always a problem. One emigrant wrote in 1843, *"An emigrant not hungry was thought to be ill."*

Pioneers found that they could resupply at a few forts along the trail, such as the one built by mountain man Jim Bridger. However, the supplies at these forts were always much more expensive than those they had bought before leaving Missouri.

Those pioneers that survived the journey to Oregon still had a lot of hard work ahead of them, but they usually found what they were looking for—an unspoiled land where they could raise their families and build a new life for themselves. As one pioneer wrote: *"I never saw so fine a population as in Oregon. They were honest, because there was nothing to steal; sober because there was no liquor; there were no misers because there was no money; they were industrious, because it was work or starve."*

Easy Simulations: Pioneers © 2008 by Tim Bailey, Scholastic Teaching Resources

Name: _____   Date: _____

CHOOSE A ROLE

Select the role that you would like to play during the pioneer simulation. Record your choice and your attributes in your diary.

Roles	Strength	Common Sense	Hunting/ Fighting Skills	Negotia-tion Skills	Medical Expertise	Health	Food	Money
Banker	2	4	1	5	3	5	2	$300
Black-smith	5	3	3	2	2	5	4	$200
Doctor	2	4	1	3	5	5	2	$250
Farmer	4	4	3	2	2	5	3	$200
Hunter	3	4	5	1	2	5	3	$200
Scout	3	5	4	2	1	5	3	$200

Banker – You have been living in the city, but are now looking for a better life in Oregon. You are skilled at negotiation and have good common sense, but are not very strong. You also bring the most money to help supply the wagon company.

Blacksmith – You are a skilled craftsman who specializes in working with metal and can repair many items that might break on the wagon. You will be very valuable in the new settlements of Oregon. Although very strong, you are not good at negotiating with people.

Doctor – You can mean the difference between life and death if a member of the wagon company falls ill or gets injured. You are highly trained in medical skills and have good common sense. But since doctors were usually older than most pioneers, you are not very strong or skilled at hunting and fighting.

Farmer – Being a skilled farmer is key to establishing a successful homestead once the company reaches Oregon. You are strong and have good common sense, but you are a poor negotiator and lack medical skills.

Hunter – You represent the kind of mountain man who knows how to live off the land in this harsh environment. A wagon company probably cannot carry all the food it will need for the journey. Therefore, a good hunter can be a great person to have along. You are, of course, very skilled at hunting and have good common sense. But because you are a loner, you have poor negotiating and medical skills.

Scout – You used to serve in the army and have led groups of people from back East to the settlements along the Mississippi River. You are very familiar with frontier life and are a skilled hunter and fighter. While you have excellent common sense, you are weak at negotiation and medical skills.

A PIONEER'S DIARY

Pioneer's Name: _____

Pioneer's Role: _____

Wagon Company's Name: _____

_____

Pioneer's Attributes:

Strength: _____

Common Sense: _____

Hunting/Fighting Skills: _____

Negotiation Skills: _____

Medical Expertise: _____

Health: _____

Pounds of food eaten per day: _____

Starting funds: _____

Name: _____ Date: _____

Date _____

Dear Diary,

_____

_____

_____

_____

_____

_____

_____

_____

_____

_____

_____

_____

_____

WAGON COMPANY JOURNAL

Wagon Company Name: _____

Wagon Company Members:

Name   Role

1. _____   _____

2. _____   _____

3. _____   _____

4. _____   _____

5. _____   _____

Money: _____   Pounds of supplies carried: _____

Pounds of food bought: _____   Pounds of food used per day: _____

Wagon type: _____

Livestock team: _____

Supplies: _____

_____

_____

_____

_____

_____

_____

_____

(continued)

WAGON COMPANY JOURNAL (continued)

Wagon Company Name: _____

Date	Number of Days Traveled	Pounds of Food Left	Pounds of Supplies Carried	Money Left
May 1, 1849				

WAGON SUPPLIES

Wagons (choose one)

*Prairie schooner – $90
The prairie schooner was a wooden wagon with a canvas cover that was waterproofed with linseed oil and provided about 5 feet of headroom. The wagon resembled a ship moving across a prairie ocean. It was approximately 10 feet long and 4 feet wide and could carry up to 2,500 pounds of cargo.

OR

*Modified farm wagon – $60
A modified farm wagon is an ordinary wagon that has been reinforced to withstand the rigors of the long trip to Oregon. However, this 10-foot-by-4-foot wagon cannot carry as much cargo as a prairie schooner due to the extra weight of the added reinforcement. It can carry only up to 2,000 pounds of cargo.

Livestock (choose one)

*Oxen team (two teams required) – $100 per team
An oxen team is made up of two oxen that are yoked together to pull a wagon. Oxen are slow-moving animals but very sturdy. They can feed off of the prairie grass as long as it's available. In an emergency, the oxen can be eaten (400 pounds of food per ox). With two teams of oxen pulling the wagon, it can travel 10 miles per day.

OR

*Mule team (two teams required) – $180 per team
A mule team is made up of two mules that are harnessed together to pull a wagon. Mules are much faster than oxen and are very durable. They require feed to be brought on the wagon for them. Each mule eats two pounds of feed per day (a total of eight pounds a day for two teams of mules). With two teams of mules pulling the wagon, it can travel 20 miles per day.

Easy Simulations: Pioneers © 2008 by Tim Bailey, Scholastic Teaching Resources

WAGON SUPPLIES (continued)

Supplies

*Food – $.25 per pound
Includes flour, bacon, coffee, cornmeal, hardtack, dried beans, dried beef, dried fruit, eggs, rice, molasses, sugar, salt, and pepper

*Water barrel – $4 (500 lbs)
A 40-gallon wooden barrel full of water

*Animal feed – $.10 per pound
Required only if mule teams are used

*Cooking gear – $8 (20 lbs)
Includes a Dutch oven, kettle, skillet, and coffee pot

*Tent – **$7** (40 lbs)
Includes the tent, poles, stakes, and anchor ropes

*Bedding – $5 (20 lbs)
Includes blankets, ground coverings, and pillows

Spare axle – $20 (200 lbs)
Can be used to replace either of the axles that the wheels attach to

Spare wagon wheel – $25
(100 lbs) Can be used to replace any of the four wheels

Spare wagon wheel spoke – $3
(5 lbs) Can be used to repair a broken wagon-wheel spoke

Spare lynch pins and bolts – $5
(5 lbs) Various parts to replace broken wagon pins and bolts

Spare yoke or harness – $10
(25 lbs) Used to attach the wagon team to the wagon

Spare livestock shoe – $2
(2 lbs) Used to shoe the animals and prevent injury

Spare wagon tongue – $15
(100 lbs) Used to connect the wagon team to the wagon

Spare wagon cover – $20
(25 lbs) A canvas covering over the top of the wagon

Heavy blanket – $2
(5 lbs) A heavy wool blanket made for cold weather

Blacksmith tools – $40
(150 lbs) Metalworking tools, including a small anvil, hammer, tongs, and bellows

Carpenter tools – $40
(50 lbs) Woodworking tools, including a saw, chisels, and auger

Farming tools – $40 (200 lbs)
Includes a plow, shovel, hoe, spade, and ax

Rifle – $50 (10 lbs) A single-shot hunting rifle

Chain – $5 (50 lbs) 20 feet of heavy chain

Rope – $5 (30 lbs) 200 feet of strong rope

Pistol – $30 (5 lbs) Can be used for self-defense but not for hunting

Bullets – $3 per box (3 lbs)
One box of bullets is used per hunt

Seed – $10 (50 lbs) Seed for planting crops in Oregon

Sewing Kit – $2 (1 lb)
Needles, scissors, and thread

Sewing Machine – $25 (40 lbs)
Foot treadle design

Linen Cloth – $10 (20 lbs)
A bolt of cloth for making clothes

Plant Cuttings – $25 (50 lbs) Fruit trees for planting in Oregon

School Books – $15 (20 lbs)
A variety of books to teach reading and writing

Lantern – $5 (5 lbs) An oil lantern

Iron Stove – $25 (150 lbs) An iron stove for heating and cooking

Banjo – $10 (5 lbs) A stringed instrument

Harmonica – $2 (1 lb) A musical instrument

Silverware – $15 (10 lbs) Finely made forks, knives, and spoons

China – $40 (20 lbs) Delicate porcelain dishes

* required item to purchase

Name: _____   Date: _____

RUBRIC #1
STUDENT'S DIARY

1 — Student did not record any events that occurred during the simulation.

2 — Student recorded very little about what occurred during the simulation.

3 — Student recorded information about what occurred during the simulation but in an incomplete fashion.

4 — Student recorded all of the important occurrences of the day's simulation, but not in a first-person narrative style.

5 — Student wrote detailed facts about the occurrences during the simulation and embellished these with personal thoughts in a believable first-person narrative style.

Score: _____

RUBRIC #2
TEACHER OBSERVATIONS

1 — Student was disruptive and prevented others from being able to participate in the simulation.

2 — Student did not participate in group discussions or simulation activities. Student might have been argumentative or disrespectful to other members of the group.

3 — Student either monopolized the group discussions or participated at a minimal level.

4 — Student participated well in the activity and allowed others to participate as well.

5 — Student was gracious in his or her participation and encouraged others to become engaged as well. Student role-played parts of the simulation to the best of his or her abilities.

Score: _____

RUBRIC #3
GROUP DYNAMICS

1 — Very poor. Members were fighting, sullen, ineffective.

2 — Poor. Members were arguing and generally ineffective, although they may have accomplished some of the simulation's tasks.

3 — Adequate. No real arguing or put-downs of group members but not very supportive of one another. The simulation's tasks were completed by the group.

4 — Good. Effective use of group time and good support of group members.

5 — Great. Fantastic group participation as well as support from group members of one another. Group members all felt free to participate and contribute their ideas.

Score: _____

Total score: _____

Easy Simulations: Pioneers © 2008 by Tim Bailey, Scholastic Teaching Resources

SIMULATION SPINNER

DIRECTIONS:

Use this spinner at various points during the simulation to determine the outcome of a situation.

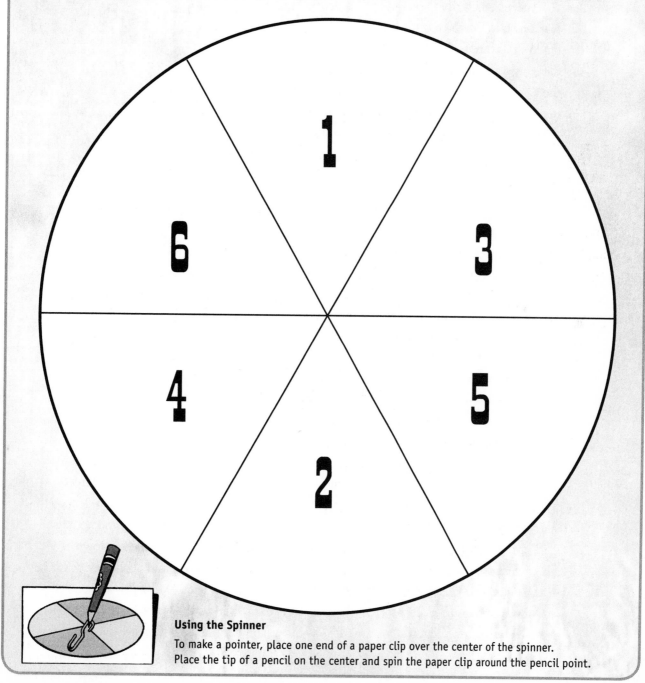

Using the Spinner

To make a pointer, place one end of a paper clip over the center of the spinner.
Place the tip of a pencil on the center and spin the paper clip around the pencil point.

Episode 1

WAGONS HO!

OVERVIEW

Students get ready to set out from Independence, Missouri, on the morning of May 1, 1849, and head out West toward a new life. (Make sure students use this date to start their diaries and journals.) They will encounter their first obstacle, the Big Blue River, and make their first major decision as traveling pioneers. Then they will rest at Fort Kearney and meet a colorful, snake-oil salesman.

Gather students together and read aloud the following passage before they embark on their journey:

May 1, 1849

It is a cool morning in the bustling town of Independence, Missouri. Early risers trample the muddy streets, watching as several pioneers make last-minute preparations before setting out on the 2,000-mile journey to the rich farmlands of Oregon or the goldfields of California. The time is right to set off for your new home. Popular guidebooks that offer advice on how best to make the crossing to Oregon declare that you should wait until the prairie grass has grown enough to feed your livestock during the journey. However, you don't want to set out too late or you risk getting snowed in trying to cross the Cascade Mountains into Oregon. As an 1849 guidebook warned, *"In prosecuting this journey, the emigrant should never forget that it is one in which time is everything."* You and your wagon company are loaded, packed, and ready to set off. With a sharp "Ha!" the reins are snapped and your wagon starts rolling away from town and from the rising sun. Friends in town as well as other pioneers preparing to leave soon wave good-bye and wish you luck. The emotions of leaving the relative civilization of Independence, Missouri, and entering the Unorganized Territory to the west were expressed by emigrant John East when he cried out, "Farewell to America" as his wagon caravan set out in 1843.

SCENARIO 1: CROSSING BIG BLUE

Have pioneers join their respective wagon companies, then read aloud the following passage:

You have traveled 160 miles to reach the Big Blue River, a tributary of the Kansas River. **(Calculate how many days it took your wagon company to reach this point and subtract the appropriate amount of food from your supplies.)** The river is deep and wide. A small wooden building stands where the trail meets the river's edge, and a large wooden ferryboat bobs next to a rough pier jutting out into the river. The ferryman, a large bearded fellow, waves and smiles as your wagon approaches. Now you must find a way to cross the river. Each wagon company has three choices:

1. Use the ferry to cross the river. The ferryman is charging $15 to cross the river.

2. Ask the ferryman for another way to cross the river.

3. Float your wagon across the river.

Allow pioneers to discuss their options within their own groups. Then invite a spokesperson from each wagon company to tell you the group's choice, making sure to take note of it on a piece of paper. After all of the wagon companies have made their decision, read them the following results:

1. If you choose to use the ferry, the wagon company can pay the $15 or negotiate for a better price. If you wish to negotiate, choose a person with good Negotiation Skills from your group to spin the spinner:

- If the person spins a number equal to or lower than his Negotiation number, your group has successfully worked out a better deal and has to pay only $10.

- If the person spins a number higher than his Negotiation Skills number, then he has offended the ferryman. You now have to pay $20 to take the ferry.

2. If you ask the ferryman for another way to cross the river, he'll tell you about a ford where you can cross the river. The ford is 40 miles to the south at a place called Alcove Spring. **If your group chooses this alternative, then you will have to travel a total of 80 miles out of your way to get back to the trail again. Calculate how many days you traveled and subtract the appropriate amount of food from your supplies.**

> ### IT'S A FACT!
> Operating ferries for pioneers could be a profitable business. During the 1850s one ferry earned more than $65,000 in just one spring.

3. If you decide to float your wagon across the river, brace yourselves. Pioneers have had to take this hazardous venture in order to cross rivers. Your wagon company must make three skill spins:

a) First, a member of your wagon company must make a Common Sense spin to remember to caulk the wagon and do it well so that it won't take on water while crossing the river:

- If the person spins a number equal to or lower than her Common Sense number, your group has done a great job of caulking the wagon.

- If the person spins a number higher than her Common Sense number, she must spin again. Multiply the number spun by 20; this is the number of pounds of food that were lost when the wagon floundered in the river. Subtract this amount from your supplies.

b) The second spin is a Strength spin to help the animals cross the river. Choose another member of the company to make the spin:

- If the person spins a number equal to or lower than his Strength number, the animals make it across the river without incident.

- If the person spins a number higher than his Strength number, the animals have been injured. If your animals are mules, water has gotten into their ears and one of the mule teams has drowned. The wagon moves at 10 miles per day until another team can be purchased. If the animals are oxen, one of the oxen misstepped in the river and injured its leg. The wagon train must rest the oxen for two days. Subtract the appropriate amount of food from your supplies.

c) The last skill spin must be made by all but one member of the wagon company. The one member who doesn't spin is driving the wagon. The rest are swimming or hanging onto the wagon while it crosses. Each swimmer must make a Strength spin:

- If a person spins a number equal to or lower than her Strength number, she has made it across the river successfully.

- If a person spins a number higher than her Strength number, she has been injured and loses one Health point for the remainder of the trip unless someone else can look at her and make a Medical Expertise spin. If this other person spins a number equal to or lower than his Medical Expertise number, the injured person regains her Health point back. Otherwise, her Health remains one point down. (Other members of the wagon company can try a Medical Expertise spin until one succeeds. Remember, skill spins can be tried only once per person.)

After successfully crossing the Big Blue River, the wagon companies are ready to continue on their journey.

SCENARIO 2: THE SNAKE-OIL SALESMAN

Read aloud the following passage:

The wagon trail has followed the wide, slow-moving Platte River for miles. The river is a brown silt-filled waterway, so muddy that it is nearly unfit to drink. **Your wagon company has covered another 240 miles and has now reached Fort Kearney. (Calculate how many days you have traveled and subtract the appropriate amount of food.)** Located near the Platte River, Fort Kearney is a collection of wooden buildings where all sorts of people, from Native Americans who live in the area to fur trappers and snake-oil salesmen, gather together.

Just as in any fort, emigrants can buy provisions from the various stores in Fort Kearney. However, any supplies purchased at these stores now cost twice as much as they did at Independence, Missouri. Emigrants may also sell any supplies that they do not want, but for only half of what they paid for the item. (This buying and selling can be done at any of the forts in this simulation.)

While at the fort, your wagon company meets Professor Thaddeus P. Farnsworth, a snake-oil salesman who offers you Professor Farnsworth's Miracle Elixir, which he claims can cure cholera, snakebite, and the common cold. The small green bottles of smelly liquid are $3 each. Each pioneer can choose from the following options:

1. You decide to pass and not buy Professor Farnsworth's Miracle Elixir.

2. You want to buy this Miracle Elixir, so you negotiate a price.

3. You're eager to try the Miracle Elixir, so you buy it and drink some.

Encourage each pioneer to tell you his or her choice, making sure to take note of it on a piece of paper. After all of the pioneers have made their decision, read them the following results:

1. If you decide to pass, you're a lot smarter than you look!

2. If you choose to negotiate a price, make a Negotiation skill spin to see what price you can get:

- If you spin a number equal to or lower than your Negotiation Skills number, Professor Farnsworth will sell you a bottle for $2.

- If you spin a number higher than your Negotiation number, he will sell you a bottle for $3.

3. If you choose to buy the stuff and drink it, you'll need to make a Negotiation Skills spin as in #2. After you've bought your bottle, go ahead and take a sip. Feel any different? With your head spinning and your stomach churning, you'll now have to reduce your Health by one point, unless someone else in your group can make a successful Medical Expertise spin:

- If this other person spins a number equal to or lower than her Medical Expertise number, you regain your Health point back.

- If this other person spins a number higher than her Medical Expertise number, your Health point remains down by one point.

DIARY PROMPT

Have students write about their travels so far. Remind them to write in character.

Episode 2

CROSSING THE PLAINS

OVERVIEW

Students attempt another river crossing, this time at the Platte River, and then endure severe weather on the open prairie.

SCENARIO 1: CROSSING THE PLATTE RIVER

Group pioneers with their own respective wagon companies and read aloud the following passage:

After resting in the relative comfort of Fort Kearney, your wagon company is ready to set out again. The day starts out very hot and humid, and after hours of walking in the oppressive heat you feel drained and wind whipped. Day after day, the open prairie rolls slowly by as your wagon travels toward the ford that crosses the muddy Platte River. **You travel 100 miles to reach the ford. (Calculate how many days you have traveled and subtract the appropriate amount of food from your supplies.)** Now, you face a dangerous crossing of the Platte River, which is running high. You have two options:

1. Wait and hope that the river level will drop so that you can ford the river without having to float your wagon across.

2. Try to cross the river now by floating your wagon across.

Allow pioneers to discuss their options within their own groups. Then invite a spokesperson from each wagon company to tell you the group's choice, making sure to take note of it on a piece of paper. After all of the wagon companies have made their decision, read them the following results:

1. If you decide to wait for the river to drop, choose a person from your wagon company to make a spin to see when the river will drop:

If you spin . . .	This happens . . .
1 or 2	The river drops after one day. Subtract one day's worth of food.
3 or 4	The river drops after two days. Subtract two days' worth of food.
5 or 6	The river drops after three days. Subtract three days' worth of food.

2. If you decide to float your wagon across the river, then steel yourselves. Just as when crossing the Big Blue River (page 30), your wagon company must make three skill spins. Remember, skill spins can be tried only once per person.

   a) First, a member of your wagon company must make a Common Sense spin to remember to caulk the wagon and do it well so that it won't take on water while crossing the river:

   - If the person spins a number equal to or lower than her Common Sense number, your group has done a great job of caulking the wagon.

   - If the person spins a number higher than her Common Sense number, she must spin again. Multiply the number spun by 20; this is the number of pounds of food that were lost when the wagon floundered in the river. Subtract this amount from your supplies.

   b) The second spin is a Strength spin to help the animals cross the river. Choose another member of the company to make the spin:

   - If the person spins a number equal to or lower than his Strength number, the animals make it across the river without incident.

   - If the person spins a number higher than his Strength number, the animals have been injured. If your animals are mules, water has gotten into their ears and one of the mule teams has drowned. Your wagon moves at 10 miles per day until another team can be purchased. If the animals are oxen, one of the oxen misstepped in the river and injured its leg. Your wagon train must rest the oxen for two days. Subtract the appropriate amount of food from your supplies.

   c) The last skill spin must be made by all but one member of the wagon company. The one member who doesn't spin is driving the wagon. The rest are swimming or hanging onto the wagon while it crosses. Each swimmer must make a Strength spin:

- If a person spins a number equal to or lower than her Strength number, she has made it across the river successfully.

- If a person spins a number higher than her Strength number, she has been injured and loses one Health point for the remainder of the trip unless someone else can look at her and make a Medical Expertise spin. If this other person spins his Medical Expertise number or lower, then the injured person regains her Health point back. Otherwise, her Health remains one point down. (Other members of the wagon company can try a Medical Expertise spin until one succeeds. Remember, skill spins can be tried only once per person.)

After crossing the Platte River, your wagon heads toward some of the most recognizable landmarks on the Oregon Trail. First, you reach Court House Rock, a 400-foot-high mound of clay and rock that was described by emigrants as looking like "a courthouse in St. Louis, or a cathedral in ruins" or "the Capitol in Washington." Next your wagon company passes Chimney Rock, a rock formation that stretches more than 500 feet into the blue prairie sky.

Chimney Rock

Courthouse Rock

SCENARIO 2: LIGHTNING, THUNDER, AND POUNDING HAIL

Read aloud the following passage to pioneers:

Your wagon rolls on across the open prairie, passing Scott's Bluff and a prairie-dog city that stretches as far as the eye can see. Fluffy white clouds drift in from the west, but soon they begin to build and darken. Within minutes they take on a frightening gray-green cast, and the wind begins to whip up in earnest.

Each wagon company needs to choose someone from their group to make a Common Sense skill spin to see how the company will deal with this nasty weather:

- If the person spins a number equal to or lower than his Common Sense number, the wagon company has decided to tie down the wagon and secure the livestock. Go to the "Ready for the Storm" table (page 36).

(continued on next page)

In the summer of 1846, Francis Parkman wrote: *"Such sharp and incessant flashes of lightning, such stunning and continuous thunder I had never known before."*

(continued)

- If the person spins a number higher than his Common Sense number, the wagon company continues on its way, unaware of how dangerous a prairie storm can be. Go to the "Not Ready for the Storm" table (page 37).

The wind continues to build, and soon blinding lightning flashes across the entire sky, followed by pounding hail. At first the hail is pea-sized, but soon they become as large as hens' eggs.

Ready for the Storm

Each wagon company makes one spin.

If you spin . . .	This happens . . .	Do this . . .
1 or 2	Frightening Lightning	Lightning spooks the livestock. Choose a pioneer to make a Common Sense spin to keep the animals calm: • If she spins a number equal to or lower than her Common Sense number, the livestock do not try to run away. • If she spins a number higher than her Common Sense number, two other people must spin their Strength number or lower to keep the animals from running. If one or both of the Strength spins fail, then the wagon company has lost an animal and must spend two days finding it.
3 or 4	Pelting Hail	Randomly choose a pioneer from the group to make a Common Sense spin to find shelter from the bruising hail: • If he spins a number equal to or lower than his Common Sense number, the pioneer has found cover under the wagon while the storm passes. • If he spins a number higher than his Common Sense number, the person must subtract 1 from his Health number. To regain the Health point, someone else must spin a number equal to or lower than her own Medical Expertise number.
5 or 6	Lost Supplies	Wind and hail have destroyed food supplies. Choose someone to make a spin. Multiply the number spun by 10 to determine how many pounds of food were lost.

Not Ready for the Storm

Each wagon company must spin twice. (The same result may be spun twice.)

If you spin . . .	This happens . . .	Do this . . .
1	Frightening Lightning	Lightning spooks the livestock. Choose a pioneer to make a Common Sense spin to keep the animals calm: • If she spins a number equal to or lower than her Common Sense number, the livestock does not try to run away. • If she spins a number higher than her Common Sense number, three other people must spin their Strength number or lower to keep the animals from running. If any of the Strength spins fail, then the wagon company has lost an animal and must spend two days to round it up.
2	Pelting Hail	Randomly choose three pioneers from the group to make Common Sense spins to find shelter from the hail: • If a person spins a number equal to or lower than his Common Sense number, that pioneer has found cover under the wagon. • If a person spins a number higher than his Common Sense number, that person has to subtract 1 from his Health number. To regain the Health point, someone else must spin a number equal to or lower than her own Medical Expertise number.
3 or 4	Lost Supplies	Wind and hail have destroyed food supplies. Choose someone to make a spin. Multiply the number spun by 20 to determine how many pounds of food were lost.
5	Wagon Blown Over	A great gust of wind up to 80 miles per hour has tipped over the wagon. Each pioneer in the group must make a Common Sense spin to determine the extent of his or her injury: • If a person spins a number equal to or lower than her Common Sense number, nothing happens to her. • If a person spins a number higher than her Common Sense number, that person loses 2 Health points. To regain 1 Health point, someone else must spin a number equal to or lower than his own Medical Expertise number to help the injured pioneer. In addition, a spin must be made to see how much food was lost. Multiply the number spun by 20 to determine how many pounds of food were lost.
6	Stampede	The livestock have bolted due to the pain of the hail and the ear-splitting thunder. Each pioneer in the group must make two spins—a Common Sense spin and a Strength spin: • If a person spins a number equal to or lower than his Common Sense number, and again equal to or lower than his Strength number, then that person has prevented one of the animals from bolting. • If a person spins a number higher than his Common Sense number or his Strength number, then an animal has run away. The wagon company must spend two days for every animal lost to round them up.

After all the wagon companies have determined their fate and calculated their damages, read aloud this passage:

Soon your wagon company is back on the trail again and is now approaching Fort Laramie. **You have traveled 140 miles. (Calculate how many days you have traveled, including any days lost during this episode, and subtract the appropriate amount of food.)** According to J.M. Shively's guidebook for the Oregon Trail, although *"you are now 640 miles from Independence, . . . it is discouraging to tell you that you have not yet traveled one third of the long road to Oregon."*

At Fort Laramie, your wagon company can resupply at twice the cost of goods as in Independence.

DIARY PROMPT

Have students write about the dramatic events in this episode. Encourage them to elaborate on how they feel about the journey, making sure to remind them to write in character.

JOURNEY TO SOUTH PASS

OVERVIEW

As students ascend the Rocky Mountains, they stumble upon a seemingly harmless stranger, who turns out to be infected with the potentially fatal disease cholera. Soon after, they meet a group of Shoshone Indians. Will this be a friendly encounter—or a deadly one?

SCENARIO 1: EXPOSED TO CHOLERA

Group pioneers with their respective wagon companies and read aloud the following passage:

After leaving Fort Laramie, your wagon company begins the steady climb into the Rocky Mountains. The land ahead looks green and lush, but as you get closer to the mountains you realize that what you thought were green meadows is actually sagebrush covering an expanse of sand and poisonous alkali springs. William Henry Russell, who came this way in 1846, disagreed with others who praised the spectacular beauty of the Rocky Mountains. Instead he wrote: *"It may captivate mad poets, but I swear I see nothing to admire."*

The steep climb is a great strain on your wagon's animal team. **If your wagonload is greater than 2,000 pounds, then for the next 260 miles, your wagon can travel only five miles per day with oxen teams or ten miles a day with mule teams. (Calculate how many days you have traveled and subtract the appropriate amount of food.)**

Along the trailside, you see various abandoned items dropped by other wagons to lighten their loads—a rusty anvil, a sheet-iron stove, even a claw-foot bathtub. You spot a man picking among these and many other abandoned items. He is collecting castoffs from other passing wagons to take back to Fort Laramie to sell. He flags down your wagon. He doesn't look well. He is dressed in ragged buckskins, and his face is pale and thin. He asks your wagon company if you have any items that you would like to get rid of to lighten your wagon. He advises you to get the wagon as light as possible for the climb to South Pass. If your wagon company wishes to give the man anything he will take it, but he has nothing to trade with you.

Unfortunately, this man has contracted cholera and has now exposed the wagon company to the disease. Each member of your wagon train needs to make a spin to see if anyone has contracted cholera:

1. If a person spins a number equal to or lower than her Health number, she did not catch the disease.

2. If a person spins a number higher than her Health number, she has been infected with cholera. The person must subtract 2 points from her Health number and spin again:

   - If she spins her Health number or lower, she has recovered. However, she must keep this lower Health number unless someone else in the wagon company can make a successful Medical Expertise spin (spin his Medical Expertise number or lower), in which case one Health point is restored.

   - If she spins a number higher than her Health number, she subtracts another 2 points from her Health number and spins again. If she fails or runs out of Health points, then she has died.

SCENARIO 2: MEETING THE SHOSHONE

Read aloud the following passage:

Your wagon rolls on into the Rocky Mountains. **After traveling 160 miles you reach Independence Rock. (Calculate how many days you have traveled and subtract the appropriate amount of food.)** Thousands of names have been written or chiseled into this rock. Your wagon company walks over to add their names to what an 1841 missionary called "The Great Record of the Desert."

(continued on next page)

Suddenly you hear a sound behind you and turn to see half a dozen Shoshone Indians on horseback. Carrying spears and tomahawks, they slowly approach your group. Your wagon company has three options:

Independence Rock

1. Run to the wagon and grab your guns.

2. Run to the wagon and try to get away.

3. Walk up to the Shoshone and try to talk to them.

Allow pioneers to discuss their options within their own groups. Then invite a spokesperson from each wagon company to tell you the group's choice, making sure to take note of it on a piece of paper. After all of the wagon companies have made their decision, read them the following results:

1. If you choose to run to the wagon and grab your guns, the Shoshone react by raising their spears and kicking their horses into a gallop. To fire at the Shoshone, each person must make a Hunting/Fighting skill spin:

- If a person spins his Hunting/Fighting number or lower, he has shot one of the Shoshone.

- If a person spins a number higher than his Hunting/ Fighting number, he has missed.

The Shoshone will attack everyone in the wagon company if they are shot at. For each Shoshone who has not been shot, a random wagon-company member must make a spin:

- If a person spins 4 or lower, then she is injured and must subtract 3 from her Health number. Otherwise, she is safe for the time being.

This entire sequence is repeated until either four of the Shoshone have been shot or everyone in the wagon company has died. After four of their people have been shot, then the Shoshone ride away.

2. If you choose to try to get away on the wagon, the Shoshone ride up alongside your wagon and seem amused that the pioneers would be trying to outrun a horse with a wagon. At this point, decide if your wagon company will try to talk with the Shoshone or fight with them.

- If your company decides to fight, see number 1 on the previous page.

- If you decide to talk with the Shoshone, see number 3, below.

3. If you take this option, walk up to the Shoshone and try to talk to them. The leader of the Shoshone seems irritated and gestures that your wagon should turn around and go back the way it came. You can either do what the Shoshone leader demands or try to negotiate with the Shoshone:

- If your wagon company decides to do what the Shoshone leader demands, then you lose five days until the Shoshone move on and you can continue down the trail. (Subtract the appropriate amount of food.)

- If you try to negotiate with the Shoshone, choose someone from your group to make a Negotiation spin.

  → If the person spins his Negotiation Skills number or lower, then your wagon company can continue on its way, but only if you give the Shoshone one of the following: a gun, five boxes of bullets, or items that are worth a total of $40. The Shoshone also have food and will trade the pioneers' supplies for food at five pounds for a dollar's worth of supplies. For example, a blanket is worth $2. It can be traded for 10 pounds of food. If at any time the pioneers become hostile, then refer to number 1 on the previous page.

  → If the person spins a number higher than his Negotiation Skills number, then you'll have to do what the Shoshone leader demands (see above).

After leaving Independence Rock, your wagon moves up the east slope of the Rocky Mountains. The mornings are chilly and the nights are cold as you reach 7,000 feet in elevation. **Finally, after 100 miles you have reached the top of the Continental Divide, South Pass in the Wind River Mountains. (Calculate how many days it took to travel and subtract the appropriate amount of food.)** From now on, all the rivers you cross flow west to the Pacific Ocean. South Pass itself is a broad meadow, some 20 or so miles wide. Crossing through the pass is one of the easier parts of the journey thus far.

INTO THE OREGON TERRITORY

OVERVIEW

Students decide whether to stop by Fort Bridger to resupply their wagon or take a shortcut through Sublette Cutoff on their way to Fort Hall. Soon after they leave Fort Hall, they follow a dangerous, rough trail through Snake River and the Blue Mountains, which takes its toll on the wagon.

SCENARIO 1: DECISION TIME

Group pioneers with their respective wagon companies and read aloud the following passage:

As you leave South Pass, your wagon company begins the gentle descent into the Oregon Territory. But you're still a long way from the fertile farmland of the Willamette Valley. **After traveling for another 20 miles (calculate how many days you have traveled and subtract the appropriate amount of food)**, the wagon company must make a decision. The guidebook says that to the south is Fort Bridger, home and namesake of mountain man Jim Bridger. This is a good place to resupply and even get a fresh team of animals. However, the guidebook suggests that this may be a waste of time and nearly 100 miles can be saved if the wagon company heads due west using the Sublette Cutoff instead of detouring to Fort Bridger. Which route will you take?

1. Stop by Fort Bridger

2. Take the Sublette Cutoff

Allow pioneers to discuss their options within their own groups. Then invite a spokesperson from each wagon company to tell you the group's choice, making sure to take note of it on a piece of paper. After all of the wagon companies have made their decision, read them the following results:

1. Stop by Fort Bridger

If your wagon company decides to take the trail to Fort Bridger, you will find it fairly easy traveling with plenty of fresh water and abundant game animals for hunting. If your company decides to hunt, double the amount of food gained per successful hunting try. (See "Hunting for Food," page 10.) **It is 40 miles to Fort Bridger. Calculate how many days you have traveled and subtract the appropriate amount of food.**

Once you reach Fort Bridger, you see what Joel Palmer described in 1844 as *"a shabby concern built of poles and daubed with mud"*—not quite what you might expect to see in a "fort." A leathery-faced man walks toward you with a smile on his face and introduces himself as Jim Bridger. He tells you that he has all the supplies that you may need (double Independence prices) and will also swap your tired, run-down animals for "recruited" oxen. These are oxen that other pioneers have traded with him in the past. He has fed and nursed them back to full strength in order to trade them with the next wagon company that comes through. This can be done for only $5 an animal. Do you want to swap your animals? (Encourage students to discuss within their own groups and then tell you their decision before reading on.)

- **If your wagon company decides to trade animals, you can reach Fort Hall in only 15 days. Subtract the appropriate amount of food.**

- **If your wagon company decides to keep your animals, it will take you 20 days to travel the 200 miles. Subtract the appropriate amount of food.**

2. Take the Sublette Cutoff

According to the guidebook, your wagon company can save nearly 100 miles by taking this shortcut. **After traveling for 20 miles (calculate how many days you have traveled and subtract the appropriate amount of food),** you find that this land is extremely desolate. There are no game animals to be hunted and the land is grassless and dotted with dried-up alkali lakes. Bleached bones of oxen can be seen along the trail, evidence of past pioneers who have tried their luck by taking this shortcut. In this desolate place, your group faces three challenges:

a) There is no way for the animals to forage for food, and they will be tempted to drink from the poisonous watering holes along the way. To keep the animals from drinking the poisonous water, choose someone in your group to make a Common Sense skill spin:

- If the person spins his Common Sense number or lower, your wagon company has successfully kept the animals away from the water.

- If the person spins a number higher than his Common Sense number, one of the animals has died. **The wagon moves at five miles per day if pulled by oxen or ten miles per day if pulled by mules until another animal can be bought.**

b) The next problem you need to tackle is feeding the livestock. If your wagon company has livestock feed, the wagon may continue at its normal pace. If you have no animal feed, someone from your wagon company must make a Common Sense spin each day of travel to keep one of the animals from dying:

- If the person spins her Common Sense number or lower, your wagon company has successfully kept an animal from dying.

- If the person spins a number higher than her Common Sense number, one animal has died. **The wagon moves at five miles per day if pulled by oxen or ten miles per day if pulled by mules until another animal can be bought.**

c) Finally, **after traveling 20 more miles (calculate how many days you have traveled and subtract the appropriate amount of food),** someone from your wagon company must make a Common Sense spin to navigate your way through the many winding paths in this region:

- If the person spins his Common Sense number or lower, your wagon company has successfully made its way through the maze of paths.

- If the person spins a number higher than his Common Sense number, your wagon company makes no progress that day. Someone in your group must spin again each day until either he succeeds on the spin and your wagon company finds its way back to the main trail or your company runs out of food and starves to death.

If your wagon company successfully overcomes these challenges, you can then travel the 100 miles to reach Fort Hall. (Calculate how many days you have traveled and subtract the appropriate amount of food).

Fort Hall is a collection of buildings with all the services and goods needed by westbound emigrants. Although built years ago by Nathaniel Wyeth, the fort is now owned and operated by the Hudson's Bay Company. This company encourages travelers to go on to California and not to Oregon. They tell settlers that the California route is much safer and that the trail to Oregon is one disaster after another. There are wild Indians, nothing to eat, and an icy death waiting in the Cascade Mountains. And if pioneers avoid the Cascade Mountains by choosing to run the Columbia River instead, then they face certain death trying to navigate the terrifying white water rapids. All of this may be true, but the Hudson's Bay Company is very interested in keeping settlers out of the fur-rich Oregon Territory, since its main business is fur trade. Your wagon company insists on continuing its way to Oregon. As a result, any goods you want to purchase in Fort Hall are now three times the Independence rate. However, if someone in your group makes a successful Negotiation Skills spin (spins her Negotiation number or lower), you can talk sellers back down to only double the Independence rate for goods.

SCENARIO 2: WAGON BREAKDOWN

Read aloud the following passage:

Your wagon company leaves Fort Hall and begins the very hazardous trail that follows the course of the Snake River and climbs into the Blue Mountains. At times, the trail takes you near breathtaking drop-offs hundreds of feet down into the Snake River. In addition, the rocky track makes driving the wagon a grueling and even painful experience. As your wagon bounces over the rough trail, it suffers a mishap from the abuse the wagon is taking on the rough track.

Each wagon company must choose someone from their group to spin the spinner and consult the following chart:

Wagon Mishap Table

Each wagon company makes one spin.

If you spin . . .	You have a . . .	This happens . . .
1	Broken Wagon Tongue	You hear a loud wooden snap. The wagon tongue must be repaired or replaced in order for the wagon to continue.
2	Broken Yoke or Harness	The wagon slows down. The animals begin to pull at their harnesses and tangle things up so they can no longer pull the wagon. The wooden cradle that holds the livestock together has broken. The yoke must be repaired or replaced before the wagon can continue.
3	Thrown Shoe	One of the animals begins to walk unsteadily and is acting as if there is something wrong with its leg. The animal has lost a shoe. If it's not replaced, the wagon travels at five miles per day for oxen or ten miles per day for mules.
4	Broken Spoke	You hear a loud snap, which sounds as if it came from one of the wheels. A spoke on a wheel has broken. The wagon can continue without repairing it, but a spin must be made: • If you spin a 1, 2, or 3, the wheel is okay and the wagon can continue normally. • If you spin a 4, 5, or 6, the wheel has broken. Refer to Wagon Mishap number 5 below.
5	Broken Wheel	You hear a metallic clanking. The wagon lurches to one side, spilling the driver from the wagon and shuddering to a stop as the wagon's axle digs into the dirt. The wood that the wheel is made from has dried and shrunk, and the metal band that is wrapped around the wheel has fallen off. The wheel has broken. It must be replaced or repaired before the wagon can continue.
6	Broken Linchpin	As the wagon rolls along, the driver notices that the animals are walking farther and farther away, dragging the harness gear with them but not the wagon. The linchpin that connects the front axle of the wagon to the wagon tongue has broken. It must be repaired or replaced in order for the wagon to continue.

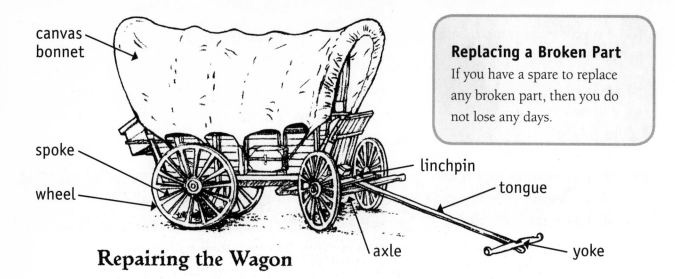

canvas bonnet

spoke

wheel

linchpin

tongue

axle

yoke

Replacing a Broken Part
If you have a spare to replace any broken part, then you do not lose any days.

Repairing the Wagon

Broken Wagon Tongue

Choose a pioneer in your group to make a Strength spin:

- If he spins his Strength number or lower, you lose two days while repairs are made. However, if the wagon company has blacksmith tools, the repairs take only one day.

- If he spins a number higher than his Strength number, the two days are lost and someone else in your group must make another spin for the repairs to be successful. This continues until a successful spin can be made (i.e., the person spins her Strength number or lower). You lose two days for each unsuccessful spin.

Broken Yoke or Harness

Choose a pioneer in your group to make a Strength spin:

- If she spins her Strength number or lower, you lose two days while repairs are made. However, if the wagon company has carpenter tools or blacksmith tools, the repairs take only one day.

- If she spins a number higher than her Strength number, the two days are lost and someone else in your group must make another spin for the repairs to be successful. This continues until a successful spin can be made (i.e., the person spins his Strength number or lower). You lose two days for each unsuccessful spin.

Thrown Shoe

Choose a pioneer in your group to make a Strength spin:

- If he spins his Strength number or lower, you lose one day while repairs are made. However, if the wagon company has blacksmith tools, the repairs do not slow down the wagon company.

- If he spins a number higher than his Strength number, the one day is lost and someone else in your group must make another spin for the repairs to be successful. This continues until a successful spin can be made (i.e., the person spins her Strength number or lower). You lose one day for each unsuccessful spin.

Broken Spoke

Choose a pioneer in your group to make a Strength spin:

- If she spins her Strength number or lower, you lose one day while repairs are made. However, if the wagon company has carpenter tools, then the repairs do not slow down the wagon company.

- If she spins a number higher than her Strength number, the one day is lost and someone else in your group must make another spin for the repairs to be successful. This continues until a successful spin can be made (the person spins his Strength number or lower). You lose one day for each unsuccessful spin.

Broken Wheel

Choose a pioneer in your group to make a Strength spin:

- If he spins his Strength number or lower, you lose three days while repairs are made. However, if the wagon company has blacksmith tools <u>or</u> carpenter tools, the repairs take only two days. If you have both sets of tools, the repairs take only one day.

- If he spins a number higher than his Strength number, the three days are lost and someone else in your group must make another spin for the repairs to be successful. This continues until a successful spin can be made (the person spins her Strength number or lower). You lose three days for each unsuccessful spin.

Broken Linchpin

Choose a pioneer in your group to make a Strength spin:

- If she spins her Strength number or lower, you do not lose any days.

- If she spins a number higher than her Strength number, the one day is lost and someone else in your group must make another spin for the repairs to be successful. This continues until a successful spin can be made (i.e., the person spins his Strength number or lower). You lose one day for each unsuccessful spin.

Remember to subtract the appropriate amount of food for any days spent making repairs. After repairs have been made on the wagon, your wagon company continues for 340 miles until you begin the steep climb into the Blue Mountains. (Calculate how many days it took to travel and subtract the appropriate amount of food.)

THE FINAL LEG OF THE JOURNEY

OVERVIEW

Students are nearing the homestretch, but they have more challenges to overcome. Depending on how long it has taken them to reach this point, pioneers may have to face a fierce winter storm in the Blue Mountains. After resting and resupplying at Fort Walla Walla, they have the option of taking the overland route through the Cascade Mountains or floating down the Columbia River. Each route has its own set of trials for the weary pioneers.

SCENARIO 1: OUTRUNNING WINTER

Group pioneers with their respective wagon companies and read aloud the following passage:

As your wagon begins its climb into the Blue Mountains, you find that the track is much rougher and harder to travel. **Your wagon company travels only 5 miles a day for the next 200 miles. (Calculate how many days you have traveled and subtract the appropriate amount of food.)** To get through the trail, you must cut down trees, clear rock slides, and wallow through thick mud, while enduring dropping temperatures as you continue to ascend the mountains.

If your wagon train has cleared this point before November 1st, then you can continue on to Fort Walla Walla without incident. However, if it's after November 1st, you get caught in a major winter storm. Refer to the "Winter Storm" table on the next page.

Winter Storm

Each wagon company makes one spin.

If you spin . . .	This happens . . .	Do this . . .
1 or 2	White Out	The snow begins falling harder and harder until you cannot see more than a few feet in front of you. If you decide to forge ahead, choose someone in your group to make a Common Sense spin to keep the wagon company from getting lost: • If he spins his Common Sense number or lower, your wagon company continues at five miles per day. • If he spins a number higher than his Common Sense number, you lose three days trying to find your way back to the trail. If you decide to wait out the storm, you lose two days before you can move on.
3 or 4	Snowed In	The snow keeps accumulating on the trail. Soon the animals are pushing it with their chests as they try to move forward. Choose two pioneers from your group to make Strength spins to keep the trail clear enough for the wagon to keep going: • If both spins succeed (each person spins her Strength number or lower), the wagon continues at five miles per day. • If either one of the spins fail, the wagon is snowed in. You must wait five days before you can continue.
5 or 6	Freezing Temperatures	The temperature has dropped well below zero with a windchill factor that could be fatal. For every heavy blanket carried by the wagon company, one person does not have to make a Health spin. Everyone else must make a Health spin: • If a person spins her Health number or lower, that person manages to keep herself warm enough. • If a person spins a number higher than her Health number, that person loses one Health point. The animals are also in danger of freezing to death. Choose someone in your group to make a Common Sense spin: • If he spins his Common Sense number or lower, your wagon company has managed to keep all of the animals alive. • If he spins a number higher than his Common Sense number, one of the animals has died and the wagon company must take an extra five days to reach Fort Walla Walla. (Subtract the appropriate amount of food without adding any extra miles.)

Once the climb over the Blue Mountains has been made, **it is a relatively easy 40 miles to Fort Walla Walla. (Calculate how many days you have traveled, including any days lost during this scenario, and subtract the appropriate amount of food).**

SCENARIO 2: FORT WALLA WALLA AND THE HOMESTRETCH

Read aloud the following passage:

> Fort Walla Walla is a fort and trading post nestled on the foothills of the Blue Mountains and near the banks of the mighty Columbia River, which flows to the Pacific Ocean. Your wagon company can resupply here (at twice the Independence rate) for the final stretch to Fort Vancouver and the Willamette Valley. However, before you set off, you have a major decision to make. There are two possible routes from here to Fort Vancouver. One is to take the overland route known as Barlow Road, which runs up and over the Cascade Mountains just south of Mt. Hood. The trail climbs over a mile in elevation and is windswept, stormy, and very hazardous, especially if the wagon company is traveling after the 1st of November. The other option is to sell the livestock, tear apart the wagon, and build a raft to float down the Columbia River. This is also a very dangerous option because this means traveling 200 miles downriver on an open raft and facing horrific rapids along the way. John Minto, an emigrant who took this route to the Willamette Valley, described it in his diary in 1844 as the most dangerous part of the entire trip to Oregon. Your wagon company must now decide which route you will take:
>
> **1.** Over the Cascade Mountains on Barlow Road
>
> **2.** Rafting the Columbia River

Allow pioneers to discuss their options within their own groups. Then invite a spokesperson from each wagon company to tell you the group's choice, making sure to take note of it on a piece of paper. After all the wagon companies have made their decision, read them the following results:

1. OVER THE CASCADE MOUNTAINS ON BARLOW ROAD

If your wagon company decides to take the overland trail, you must set out prior to November 1st. **If you do not leave before that date, you travel 120 miles (calculate how many days you traveled and subtract the appropriate amount of food) only to find that your way is blocked**

by snow in the mountain pass. You must turn back to Fort Walla Walla and take the Columbia River down to Fort Vancouver. **(Calculate 120 miles worth of days traveled back to Fort Walla Walla and subtract the appropriate amount of food.)**

If your wagon company sets out before November 1st, the route is open and you can attempt to make the crossing over the Cascade Mountains. The mountain trail is very rough, and it is a daily chore to cut and hack your way through the undergrowth and avoid rockslides and avalanches. It is also difficult to find game animals to hunt in the higher elevations. If your wagon company decides to hunt, you must stop for two days instead of the usual one for hunting. (See "Hunting for Food," page 10.) In addition, the wagon can travel only five miles a day through this wilderness for the 100-mile trip over the Cascade Range. During the trip there are several opportunities for mishaps. Choose someone in your group to spin the spinner once for every 25 miles that the wagon company travels, for a total of four times. (Choose a different person for each spin.)

- If the person spins a 1, 2, 3, or 4, refer to the "Cascade Crossing" table below.

- If the person spins a 5 or 6, then you journey through those 25 miles uneventfully.

Cascade Crossing

Make one spin for every unsuccessful spin above.

If you spin . . .	This happens . . .	Do this . . .
1 or 6	Old Landslide	A great amount of rock and dirt has fallen across the path and must be cleared before the wagon can continue. Each member of the wagon company must make a Strength spin. For every person's spin that fails (the person spins a number higher than his Strength number), you spend one day clearing the path. For instance, if two people fail their Strength spin, then the party must spend two days clearing the path without traveling.
2	Landslide!	As your wagon company passes, a landslide shakes loose from the mountain overhead. Small rocks and dirt begin falling, followed by larger boulders. Each pioneer must make a Common Sense spin. Each person that makes a successful spin (spins her Common Sense number or lower) takes cover or jumps out of the way. If a person fails the Common Sense spin, he gets hit by falling rocks and subtracts 2 from his Health number. If another pioneer makes a successful Medical Expertise spin (spins her Medical Expertise number or lower), the injured person loses only one Health point.
3	Snowstorm	Snow begins to fall and is soon blowing through the mountain pass. Two Common Sense spins must be made in order to keep the wagon on the trail. If either spin fails (a person spins a number higher than his Common Sense number), the wagon breaks a wheel. (Refer to the "Wagon Mishap" table, page 47.) If your company decides to wait out the storm, you must wait three days for the storm to blow over.

(continued on next page)

Cascade Crossing

(continued)

If you spin . . .	This happens . . .	Do this . . .
4	Tree Fall	A large tree has fallen across the trail and must either be moved or hacked through to make a path. • If you decide to try and move the tree, three pioneers must make a successful Strength spin (spin their Strength number or lower) to move the tree. If any of the three spins fail, you cannot move the tree. • If you decide to hack through the tree, the task will take three days. If your wagon company has an axe, it will take only one day. If you have carpenter tools, it will take two days.
5	Avalanche	With a resounding boom much like the sound of distant thunder from above, an avalanche begins sliding toward your wagon company. Fortunately, most of the slide misses the wagon. However, each pioneer must make a Common Sense spin to get out of the way. • If a person spins his Common Sense number or lower, he has safely gotten out of the way. • If a person spins a number higher than his Common Sense number, he must subtract one Health point. If someone else can make a successful Medical Expertise spin (spins her Medical Expertise number or lower), the injured person does not have to subtract a point. In addition to the danger to pioneers, the livestock can be caught in the racing snow. Choose someone to spin the spinner: • If the person spins a 1, 2, or 3, the animals are safe. • If the person spins a 4, 5, or 6, the animals are trapped. Two pioneers must each make a successful Strength spin (spin their Strength number or lower) to save the animals before they suffocate. For each failed Strength spin, one animal dies and the wagon company takes five extra days to go over the mountains. (Subtract the appropriate amount of food but without any miles traveled).

One last challenge remains for the wagon company as you come down out of the mountains. One section of the trail is so steep that the wagon must be slid down the slope using ropes in a controlled skid. At the bottom of the slope, you can see the splintered remains of wagons that did not survive this maneuver. First, you must unhitch the livestock and unload as much weight as possible from the wagon. Then, you must use chains to bind the wagon wheels so that they

54

cannot turn. (If you don't have chain then you can use rope, but it will not work as well.) Finally, you tie ropes to the wagon and use these to lower the wagon down the trail.

LOWERING THE WAGON DOWN THE TRAIL

Choose two pioneers from your group—one to make a Common Sense spin and another to make a Strength spin. If your wagon company does not have chain to bind the wheels, then subtract one point from each pioneer's Common Sense and Strength numbers. If you do not have rope as well, then subtract three more points from their Common Sense and Strength numbers.

For example, if a wagon company has neither chain nor rope and both people who were chosen to spin have a 5 for their Common Sense and Strength, respectively, they must subtract 1 point for having no chain and 3 points for having no rope. So instead of needing to spin a 5 or lower to succeed, they must spin a 1.

If either of the two spins fail, then the wagon company must spin three times on the Wagon Mishap Table below and deal with the consequences.

Wagon Mishap Table

Each wagon company must spin three times.

If you spin . . .	You have a . . .	This happens . . .
1	Broken Wagon Tongue	You hear a loud wooden snap. The wagon tongue must be repaired or replaced in order for the wagon to continue. This mishap can occur only once. If spun twice, then ignore and spin again.
2 or 4	Broken Spoke	You hear a loud snap, which sounds as if it came from one of the wheels. A spoke on a wheel has broken. The wagon can continue without repairing it, but a spin must be made: • If you spin a 1, 2, or 3, the wheel is okay, and the wagon can continue as normal. • If you spin a 4, 5, or 6, the wheel has broken. Refer to Broken Wheel (3 or 5) below.
3 or 5	Broken Wheel	One of the wheels shatters as it strikes a huge rock. The wheel must be replaced or repaired before the wagon can continue. This result can happen multiple times.
6	Broken Axle	The wagon smashes into a rock and you hear a deafening snap as an axle comes apart. Both wheels on the axle fall to the sides. This result can happen two times; if it happens more than that, spin again.

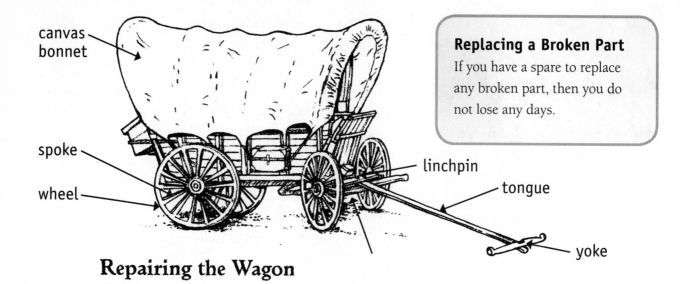

canvas bonnet

spoke

wheel

linchpin

tongue

yoke

Replacing a Broken Part
If you have a spare to replace any broken part, then you do not lose any days.

Repairing the Wagon

Broken Wagon Tongue

Choose a pioneer in your group to make a Strength spin:

- If he spins his Strength number or lower, you lose two days while repairs are made. However, if the wagon company has blacksmith tools, the repairs take only one day.

- If he spins a number higher than his Strength number, the two days are lost and someone else in your group must make another spin for the repairs to be successful. This continues until a successful spin can be made (i.e., the person spins her Strength number or lower). You lose two days for each unsuccessful spin.

Broken Spoke

Choose a pioneer in your group to make a Strength spin:

- If she spins her Strength number or lower, you lose one day while repairs are made. However, if the wagon company has carpenter tools, the repairs do not slow down the wagon company.

- If she spins a number higher than her Strength number, the one day is lost and someone else in your group must make another spin for the repairs to be successful. This continues until a successful spin can be made (i.e., the person spins his Strength number or lower). You lose one day for each unsuccessful spin.

Broken Wheel

Choose a pioneer in your group to make a Strength spin:

- If he spins his Strength number or lower, you lose three days while repairs are made. However, if the wagon company has blacksmith tools <u>or</u> carpenter tools, the repairs take only two days. If you have both sets of tools, the repairs take only one day.

- If he spins a number higher than his Strength number, the three days are lost and someone else in your group must make another spin for the repairs to be successful. This continues until a successful spin can be made (i.e., the person spins her Strength number or lower). You lose three days for each unsuccessful spin.

Broken Axle

Choose a pioneer in your group to make a Strength spin:

- If she spins her Strength number or lower, you lose four days while repairs are made. However, if the wagon company has blacksmith tools <u>or</u> carpenter tools, the repairs take only three days. If you have both sets of tools, the repairs take only two days.

- If she spins a number higher than her Strength number, the four days are lost and someone else in your group must make another spin for the repairs to be successful. This continues until a successful spin can be made (i.e., the person spins his Strength number or lower). You lose four days for each unsuccessful spin.

Remember to subtract the appropriate amount of food for any days spent making repairs.

Finally, your wagon company has crossed the Cascade Mountains. **After traveling for 20 miles, you arrive at Fort Vancouver. (Calculate how many days you have traveled and subtract the appropriate amount of food.)**

2. RAFTING THE COLUMBIA RIVER

The Columbia River is wide and deceptively calm as it flows past Fort Walla Walla. Your wagon company must tear apart your wagon and use it to build a raft to float the 200 miles to Fort Vancouver. **You need 200 feet of rope and 10 days to build the raft (subtract the appropriate amount of food).** If your wagon company does not have rope, then you'll have to buy it from another wagon company for three times its normal price. You can either use cash or trade items worth the amount needed. The raft can carry only pioneers and 1,000 pounds of cargo. (Figure out how much weight you are taking with you.) After the raft is loaded you are ready to set out. **You can travel 20 miles per day on the river.**

However, danger in the form of three sets of rapids is coming up. There is no way to avoid the rapids. You must go through them and hope for the best. **The first set of rapids is 40** miles down the river. (Calculate how many days you have traveled and subtract the appropriate amount of food.) As the raft approaches the rapids, you first hear the roar of the white water and then see the spray as the water smashes against the jagged rocks that are both jutting above the river and lying hidden beneath the waves. You work frantically

with your homemade oars to steer the raft past the most obvious perils and hope that you aren't crushed by the dangers you can't see. See the Rapids Table below. Make another spin on this table after you have traveled 120 miles and again after 180 miles.

Rapids Table

Make a spin after traveling 40 miles, then 120 miles, and again after 180 miles.

If you spin . . .	This happens . . .	Do this . . .
1	Whirlpool	The raft is caught in a whirlpool in the river. It spins the raft round and round. You lose 100 pounds of cargo (choose which items are lost) before you can clear the rapids.
2 or 5	Smashed Against the Rocks	The raft is heading for jagged rocks. Two wagon company members must each make a Strength spin to avoid smashing into the rocks: • If both pioneers spin their Strength numbers or lower, you have successfully avoided the rocks. • If either spin fails (a person spins a number higher than his Strength number), the raft has smashed into the rocks. You lose 100 pounds of cargo (choose which items are lost). In addition, randomly choose a member of the wagon company to lose two Health points. If someone else can make a successful Medical Expertise spin (spin her Medical Expertise number or lower), the injured member loses only one point.

(continued on next page)

Rapids Table

(continued)

If you spin . . .	This happens . . .	Do this . . .
3	Overboard!	A member of the wagon company is thrown overboard by the violent motion of the raft plunging though the rapids. (Randomly choose which person is thrown off the raft.) a) The person must make a successful Strength spin (spin his Strength number or lower) or lose one Health point. b) The same person can make another Strength spin to try and swim back to the raft. In addition, another member of the wagon company must make a Strength spin to try and pull the swimmer onto the raft. Both spins must succeed (spin their Strength number or lower) in order for the person to get back on the raft. If both spins fail, the person who fell overboard loses another Health point. This pattern continues until either the person is back on the raft or has lost all of his Health points and drowned. If the person makes it back on the raft, someone else in the company must make a successful Medical Expertise spin (spin her Medical Expertise number or lower) in order for the nearly drowned pioneer to regain one Health point.
4	Trough	The raft dives into a deep trough in the rapids and a great wave of water washes away food supplies. Choose someone in the group to spin the spinner. Multiply the number spun by 20; this is the number of pounds of food lost in the river. Subtract this amount from your supplies.
6	Broken Oars	As the raft lurches through the rapids, you try to steer the raft around the rocks and snags. Two pioneers from your group must each make a Common Sense spin to avoid breaking an oar on the rocks: • If they both spin their Common Sense number or lower, you get through without any problems. • If either person spins a number higher than her Common Sense number, she must make a Strength spin or be thrown overboard (see #3). If the person make a successful Strength spin (spins her Strength number or lower), the wagon company must still stop for one day to make new oars. (Subtract the appropriate amount of food).

After successfully rafting down the Columbia River, your wagon company has reached Fort Vancouver, the last stop on the Oregon Trail.

BUILDING A CABIN AND PLANTING A FARM

Read aloud the following passage:

You have finally arrived in the beautiful Willamette Valley, and it is everything that you dreamed it would be. As one pioneer described it: *"Picture an evergreen valley 150 miles long and 40 miles wide . . . the rich agricultural surface of the valley interspersed with timber and prairie in profitable proportions, and innumerable springs of pure, soft water."* The climate of the Willamette Valley is perfect for farming—warm summers that are not too hot and mild winters with plenty of rain. As noted by Peter Burnett, who emigrated to the Willamette Valley in 1843: *"The copious rains fertilize the soil of the fields and keep them always fresh and productive."* However, with all of this bounty comes a great amount of effort on the part of the pioneers. A cabin must be built and crops planted. For in addition to planting crops that will feed you and your family, you will need extra to trade for those items that you either couldn't bring with you on the trip or had to leave behind somewhere on the trail.

To see if you get off to a successful start as homesteaders, a joint Common Sense spin must be made. To determine your group's Common Sense number, average all of the surviving company members' Common Sense numbers and round up. For example, say a wagon company consists of four people and their respective Common Sense numbers are 4, 5, 2, and 4, which adds up to 15. Divide this total by the number of pioneers, 4, and round up the result, 3.75, to the nearest whole number, 4. For the Common Sense spin to be successful, a spin of 4 or lower must be made. Before making this final spin, however, consult the following table for bonuses or penalties.

Every member of the wagon company must spin this new number for the Common Sense spin. If at least half of the pioneers succeed at the spin (spins the joint Common Sense number or lower), then the new homesteaders will survive their first year in Oregon and become a part of American history.

Common Sense Bonuses and Penalties

Add 1 point to your group's Common Sense average for each of the following:

- having oxen for pulling a plow
- having farming tools
- having at least $50 to buy farming supplies
- every surviving pioneer that is a farmer

- every 50 lbs of seed
- having a plow
- having carpentry tools
- having a sewing machine

Subtract 1 point from your group's Common Sense average for:

- every member of the wagon company who has died

Final Common Sense number: _____

Wrapping Up

The day after the class has completed the simulation, invite students to write a letter to "Aunt Bertha," who lives back East, describing what they learned through their experiences during the simulation. You may either have a debriefing discussion before students write their letter to refresh their memories or have students write the letter first so they're not influenced by other people's experiences.

Read aloud the following passage:

You have settled into your new home in Oregon and you have some time to relax. Write a letter to your Aunt Bertha and tell her about your experiences over the past several months on your journey from Independence, Missouri, to the Willamette Valley of Oregon. What did you learn? What were the highlights of the experience? How did it change what you thought it would be like to travel on the Oregon Trail? Let her know all about your experience because this letter is the only way that she will ever know what it was like to be a pioneer on the Oregon Trail.

Use this letter and students' pioneer journal to assess whether or not students truly learned what it was like to be a pioneer during this period in history.

LETTER TO AUNT BERTHA

Date _____

Dear Aunt Bertha,

_____

_____

_____

_____

_____

_____

_____

_____

_____

Love,

_____

PIONEER RECIPES

To celebrate the culmination of a successful simulation, try these somewhat modernized pioneer recipes with your class:

Fried Cakes

Combine 1 ½ cups of flour with 1 cup of water. Mix well with a fork. Using plenty of flour on your hands and a breadboard, roll out the dough to a thickness of ¼ inch. Cut into 2-inch squares. Fry in beef or bacon fat. Brown slowly on both sides. Sprinkle with salt to taste. Makes about 20 cakes.

Soda Bread

To make dough, mix 1 teaspoon of baking soda with 1 cup of warm water. Add 2 ¼ cups of flour and 1 teaspoon of salt. Knead well. The dough may be used at once or allowed to rise overnight. Flatten dough to a thickness of 1 inch. Place on a greased cookie sheet and bake at 400 degrees for 25 minutes.

Mormon Johnnycake

Combine 2 cups of yellow cornmeal, ½ cup of flour, 1 teaspoon of baking soda, and 1 teaspoon of salt. Stir in 2 cups of buttermilk and 2 tablespoons of molasses. Pour into a greased 9-inch pan and bake at 425 degrees for 20 minutes.

Dried Apple Pie

Soak 2 cups of dried apples in water overnight. Drain off the water and mix apples with ½ cup sugar and 1 teaspoon each of cinnamon and allspice. Line an 8-inch pan with a premade crust, add the apple mixture, dot with 3 tablespoons of butter and cover with a second crust. Make a few slashes in the top for ventilation and bake at 350 degrees for 1 hour, until the crust is golden brown.

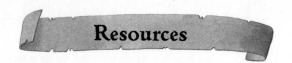

Resources

Books:

Daily Life in a Covered Wagon
by Paul Erickson (Puffin, 1997)

A Pioneer Sampler: The Daily Life of a Pioneer Family in 1840
by Barbara Greenwood (Houghton Mifflin, 1998)

Dear America: Across the Wide and Lonesome Prairie: The Oregon Trail Diary of Hattie Campbell, 1847
by Kristiana Gregory (Scholastic, 1997)

My America: Westward to Home: Joshua's Oregon Trail Diary
by Patricia Hermes (Scholastic, 2002)

Pioneer Days: Discover the Past with Fun Projects, Games, Activities, and Recipes
by David C. King (Jossey-Bass, 1997)

If You Traveled West in a Covered Wagon
by Ellen Levine (Scholastic, 1992)

Rachel's Journal: The Story of a Pioneer Girl
by Marissa Moss (Silver Whistle Books, 2001)

Primary Sources Teaching Kit: The Westward Movement
by Karen Baicker (Scholastic, 2002)

Hands-on History: Pioneers
by Michael Gravois (Scholastic, 2004)

Web Sites:

Kid Info: Pioneers and Westward Expansion
http://www.kidinfo.com/American_History/Pioneers.html

Kids Konnect – Pioneers
http://www.kidskonnect.com/content/view/276/27/

Life for the Travelers Along the Trail
http://ourworld.compuserve.com/homepages/trailofthe49ers/life.htm

The Oregon Territory and Its Pioneers
http://www.oregonpioneers.com/ortrail.htm

The Oregon Trail
http://www.isu.edu/~trinmich/Oregontrail.html

Pioneer Life in America
http://library.thinkquest.org/J001587

Pioneers
http://library.thinkquest.org/6400